ANNA P

SKEW WHIFF

Illustrated by
Tony Ross

OXFORD
UNIVERSITY PRESS

OXFORD
UNIVERSITY PRESS

Great Clarendon Street, Oxford OX2 6DP

Oxford University Press is a department of the University of Oxford.
It furthers the University's objective of excellence in research, scholarship,
and education by publishing worldwide in

Oxford   New York

Auckland   Cape Town   Dar es Salaam   Hong Kong   Karachi
Kuala Lumpur   Madrid   Melbourne   Mexico City   Nairobi
New Delhi   Shanghai   Taipei   Toronto

With offices in

Argentina   Austria   Brazil   Chile   Czech Republic   France   Greece
Guatemala   Hungary   Italy   Japan   Poland   Portugal   Singapore
South Korea   Switzerland   Thailand   Turkey   Ukraine   Vietnam

Oxford is a registered trade mark of Oxford University Press
in the UK and in certain other countries

British Library Cataloguing in Publication Data

Data available

ISBN-13: 978-0-19-915967-3
ISBN-10: 0-19-915967-X

3 5 7 9 10 8 6 4

Printed in the UK by Ashford Colour Press Ltd

Available in packs

Year 6 / Primary 7 Pack of Six (one of each book)   ISBN 13: 978-0-19-915971 0
                                                         ISBN 10: 19-915971 8

Contents

1 Huh?   5

2 Please Help me!   17

3 Problem Solved   25

4 Wonky!   42

5 In Her Dreams   59

6 YOU DID OOO-DID-OOO!   69

7 Brilliant   84

About the author   96

1
Huh?

"Two per cent for maths," Mum slapped the table with the school report. "How can a child of mine get two per cent for maths?"

Anjuli decided not to tell her that maths was the most boring subject in the world. Instead she concentrated on an amazing blob in the middle of the kitchen table and scraped away at it with her sharpest fingernail, as if her life depended on it.

"And if that isn't bad enough," Mum spat, "do you know what Mr Williams has written?"

Anjuli could imagine. She shook her

slippery black hair over her face and shrank back in the chair.

"*A higher mark than I was expecting.* That's what he's written. I can't believe it."

A smile almost crossed Anjuli's face but she stopped it just in time. Any moment the volcano would subside, then she could run next door to Pete's house and help him get his birthday tea ready.

"I really don't know what to say," Mum's arms flopped in front of her. "I give up."

Anjuli leaped to her feet as fast as she could and ran out of the back door into the pouring rain. "I'll be back after tea. You know I promised to help Pete."

A few seconds later, Anjuli poked her nose through the gate in the fence to check that Pain, Pete's dog, was safely tied up to the tree. The only tree in the whole of Elm Close.

"WHAR," she snarled at him, knowing he couldn't get her back.

"GRRRRRR," growled Pain, the black mongrel, then went back to chewing his stick.

"Leave him alone." Pete made a sucky

sound through the gaps in his huge tombstone teeth. "He's sweet as anything! Undo him, the postman's been."

"He's a killer dog and he's soaked through!" Anjuli said. "Just look at his yellow eyes. He's probably got rabies. Why don't you get him a kennel?"

"Killer dog, ha?" Pete huffed. "He runs away from cats. Pain's never killed a fly."

They had this conversation every day and Pete was getting bored with it. "You ought to see someone about your fear of dogs. And we're going to get him a kennel one of these days."

"Oh, yeah?" Anjuli followed him into his perfect house. Then she suddenly nudged Pete's side. "You lucky thing!"

She couldn't hide her jealousy at the sight of Pete's main tenth birthday present, open on the kitchen table. There in front of her was a fantastic woodwork set, complete with rows of different-sized chisels, screwdrivers, hammers and saw blades. There was even a bench plane and a selection of nails.

"I wanted a computer games system," Pete groaned. "Not a bunch of tools."

"All I got for my tenth birthday was a writing set and a packet of glow stars," Anjuli said.

"What did you get for your eleventh?" Pete asked.

"You don't want to know," Anjuli sighed. "But it had fake money and two dice!"

Today was going from bad to worse.

"It's not fair!" Anjuli could feel herself actually turning green. Just looking at those tools with their smooth wooden handles made her fingers itch.

"Well," Pete said, taking the hint. "Want to make something? We've got all day."

Anjuli rubbed the rain from her hair.

"Shouldn't we be buttering bread?"

"They're not coming till three o'clock. It's half past eight in the morning," Pete said. "Or can't you tell the time?"

"Huh?" Anjuli twitched her lips. "You're right. We can make the sandwiches later. They won't take long."

They both stared round the brand new kitchen. There was a white formica table, four plastic chairs, a fridge freezer and some cupboards painted lemon yellow.

"Nothing much to fix up here, is there?" she said, disappointed.

"Have we got time to build a bird table, like the one at number sixty-three?" Pete asked.

'Maybe." Then Anjuli had a better idea. "Your mum's been complaining about that sticking door for ages. Why don't we mend it?"

Pete turned his blue eyes towards the offending scraping door which separated the kitchen from the living room. He eyed up the scratches that the door made in the tile floor every time it was dragged back and forth.

"This door will be the death of me," Pete's mum said a million times a day.

They both listened to a loud coughing sound coming from the bedroom upstairs.

"When she's up and about after the flu, the door will be mended and she'll be dead pleased," Anjuli suggested with a sideways smile. "Yeah?"

'Mmm!" Pete twiddled his ear lobe and blinked a couple of times. Why hadn't he thought of that? Anjuli, being a year older, was always one step ahead of him and it drove him mad sometimes. "Not sure."

"Come on," Anjuli sighed. "Do something *I* want for a change!"

Pete didn't have the heart to argue. After all, she had offered to help him get his birthday tea ready now Mum was sick in bed. "OK then."

Without another word, Anjuli swished her slippery black hair out of her eyes, dragged a chair over to the pine door and climbed up, waving at Pete to pass her a screwdriver.

"Come on."

"This one?" Pete held up a small one.

"No, bigger!" she pushed it away. "There," she pointed.

Pete handed her another screwdriver and Anjuli slipped it easily into the top hinge. "Perfect fit."

"Yep!" Pete stepped back and watched carefully as the top of the door slowly loosened and started to slip away from the hinge. "That's it."

He reached up and took the screws from Anjuli, placed them carefully on the table, then leaned forward to steady the door with his hands.

Anjuli jumped down and began attacking the lower hinge like a real professional. This was the most fun she'd had in ages. The last screw came undone with just four turns. Pete staggered backwards under the weight of the wooden door as Anjuli let go.

"Yah," she jumped off the chair and threw the screwdriver and screws across the table. "We did it!"

"Aargh!" Pete yelled, bending back under the weight of the door. "Hurry up! I'm going to be crushed to death."

Anjuli quickly grabbed a corner of the door. Together they heaved it up on to the kitchen table, which was half its size. It wobbled for a second before they re-adjusted its position and stood back.

"We should put an advert in the corner shop and go into business," Anjuli sniffed like a workman. "What do you think? We could mend all the doors in Elm Close and make a fortune, then Sarky Williams, my maths teacher, would have to eat his words."

"Saw!" Pete wasn't listening. He was concentrating on the next stage of the job like a real carpenter. "Need to get that edge off and straighten it up a bit."

"Here," Anjuli handed him the shimmering blade.

Pete sawed the air above his head for a second before bending down to start cutting. But he couldn't get the blade through the wood. "It doesn't work!" he said disappointedly, after only three jabs which jarred his shoulder.

"I'll do it!" Anjuli grabbed Pete's shoulder. "You're holding it all wrong."

She took the saw from him, plunged the sharp blade into the door edge and tried to push it up and down. The saw bent, the teeth jagged. "It's this saw. Look, it's all soft and bendy. It's wobbling." She waved it around, and the blade made a *judder*, *judder* sound.

"Put it back," Pete said. "Give me the plane."

Anjuli plucked the plane from the toolbox by its beautiful rounded top and handed it to Pete as if it were a precious jewel.

"Think we should measure how much needs to come off?" she wondered.

"Nah," Pete said. "I know what I'm doing. I just need to slice off that bit there."

Anjuli sighed, wishing she could slide the plane along the bottom of the door as easily as Pete. With both hands she kept the other end of the door as steady as she could while he worked. Curls of honey-coloured wood fell to the floor as softly as newly-cut hair. The plane whooshed up and down smooth as a duster.

"Don't get carried away!" Anjuli warned. "Give us a go." She was itching to get her hands on the plane.

Pete stopped for a second. "All right," he said, arms out wide, steadying the other end of the door. "But mind you keep it even."

Anjuli grabbed the plane. It fitted her hand like a glove. It slid along the bottom of the door like a slipper on ice. She patted the newly exposed wood with her free hand. The smell was gorgeous. This was great. She forgot all about her maths report.

"That's enough!" Pete suddenly decided. "We've taken the right amount off now."

Anjuli was sad to have to stop, but she supposed he was right. "Let's get the door back on."

Mum coughed loudly upstairs. They needed to hurry up.

"You take this side!" Pete pointed.

Anjuli grabbed the shaved end of the door and between them they managed to lift it from the table and stand it up. Pete held on tight as Anjuli grabbed the screwdriver and climbed back on to the chair. She pulled the door towards her and began to screw the top hinge back into place.

"Maybe we could make a kennel next?" Anjuli suggested as she jumped down from the chair to attack the bottom hinge. She was so busy tightening the last screw she didn't notice the growing frown on Pete's face. "There you are, all finished."

They both stared at the hanging door.

2

Please Help Me!

"How did that happen?" Anjuli was shocked.

Pete was more than shocked. He was dumbfounded. A large, wedge-shaped hole had appeared from nowhere. They could clearly see the gas fire in the next room through the gap.

"We didn't take that much off!" Anjuli gasped. "Did we?"

"No..." Pete shook.

"I told you to stop," Anjuli said. "But you kept on."

"It was you with that plane! Not me." Pete glared at her. "Mum"ll go off her head. She's just had the kitchen done. It's your fault! You're always trouble, you are!"

"Stop crying! We can stick all the bits back on." Anjuli picked up a pile of wood shavings from the floor. "There's no need to get in a state. It's only a door."

Pete couldn't speak. That was the trouble with Anjuli, he decided. She just didn't know a crisis when it stared her in the face. "And I'm not crying!" He tried to explain, in his patient voice, "Later today, my moany uncle Chas, posh cousins Phil and Jen, Granny Vane and that horrible kid Luffy from number forty-eight – the one you fancy like mad – are going to be here to eat a sarny or two. And Mum might stagger down to say hello and see…"

"A door that's been done up for a birthday tea," Anjuli said. "And who says I fancy Luffy?"

Pete shrugged, "Dunno." He wasn't going to tell her.

"Who says I fancy Luffy?" She glared at him. "Well?"

"Er…" Pete looked at the sink for help. "Um… I just guessed. The way you go all silly when he's around and you giggle like a…"

"Stop!" Anjuli had had enough. "As a matter of fact, I think he's horrible. OK?"

Pete gave her a knowing smile and let the subject drop. "If that's how you want it."

"We've got plenty of time to disguise the gap and make all the food." Anjuli marched up and down the kitchen floor crossly. "I don't know why you're so worried. It just needs a bit of thought."

"It does?" Pete started to feel sick. Anjuli's ideas always went wrong. Why would the next one be any better?

"Hey, how about this?" Anjuli grabbed the Happy Birthday banner from the window sill and unrolled it. "Perfect!"

She knelt on the floor and held the banner across the gap in the door. "Hand me some sticky tape or something."

Pete opened a drawer and found a roll of

sticky tape. He handed it to her, then stood back sighing as she stuck the thing on in a wonky line.

"Why am I so brilliant?" Anjuli fell back on the floor, pleased as punch. "And nobody in the whole world knows!"

"It looks stupid," Pete said. "And how's it going to look from the living room?"

"Haven't you got another one?" Anjuli sat up. Pete shook his head. "Oh well, let's have your Manchester United scarf, then."

"Great!" Pete said crossly. "So there's a wonky birthday banner on the bottom of the door on the kitchen side and a Man United scarf on the bottom of the door on the living room side, and no one's going to think I live in a mad house, yeah?"

"Let's stick tons of things on the door so they won't look odd." Anjuli waved her arms in the air as if she couldn't wait to decorate the door. "You've got loads of posters in your bedroom. Come on, we've got the sandwiches to do and your mum asked me to make a fort out of all those fudge bars she got cheap."

"Great!" Pete said to himself as he trudged upstairs to rip his posters from the walls. "I'm ten and Mum wants me to have a fort for a cake!"

"Everything all right, darling?" Mum's croaky voice called from her bedroom. "Is that nice Anjuli here?"

"Yeah," Pete popped his head round her door. "We're decorating the kitchen door to make it more like a party. OK, Mum?" He gave her a smile to die for.

"Lovely idea," Mum nodded. "Do whatever you like to the door, darling. I just wish I could help."

"Stay there," Pete said nervously. "Fancy another hot lemon drink?" She shook her head. Pete closed the door and said a prayer, the first one he'd ever said outside Assembly. It went: "Please someone, PLEASE HELP ME! Otherwise I'm going to have to kill Anjuli."

He tore everything from his bedroom walls. A red woollen hat, two computer game posters advertising games he was desperate to own, and a photo of Granny Vane winning a line dancing competition.

"Great," Anjuli rubbed her hands together when she saw all the stuff in Pete's arms. "Let's stick it on. I"ll do the kitchen side. You do the living room side."

"Haven't you got any more sticky tape or that blue stuff?" Anjuli called after a few minutes. "This sock won't stick."

"What sock?" Pete dropped his poster on the floor and stepped into the kitchen.

"I found it in the drawer," Anjuli

explained. "It's so sweet."

"You can't put that up! It's a Christmas stocking and it's July," Pete shouted. "Why is there a poster on the door of Dead Racer with a photo of my Granny Vane line dancing along a track dripping with blood?"

Pete sighed and rescued the photo of Granny Vane in her white cowboy boots from the middle of a crashed car. "No, I haven't got any more sticky tape."

"We'd better get some," Anjuli jumped up from the floor. "I'm only half-way through. Got some money?"

Pete nodded. "If my mum comes downstairs and sees this mess…"

"Stop worrying. Let's go to the shop," Anjuli grinned.

"Near Luffy's house?" Pete gave her a sideways look. "That shop?"

"It is the nearest," Anjuli strode out of the back door. "Got a better idea?"

"Come on, Pain, want a walkie?" Pete nuzzled Pain's wet nose, undid the leash and let the dog smother his jeans with saliva. "Wait up," Pete attached the lead to Pain's collar and ran as fast as he could after Anjuli.

When he turned the corner he saw Luffy leaning against the Cherry Avenue sign with Anjuli. He was cackling like a maniac, throwing chips from a newspaper into the air and catching them one by one in his gaping mouth.

"How can you scoff those at nine o'clock in the morning?" Pete shouted.

3

Problem Solved

"Have one." Luffy unfolded his rake-thin, rag-bag body and held out the packet of chips to Pete.

"They're delish," Anjuli said to Pete with a silly look on her face. "Go on. I've had one!"

"At this time of day?" Pete frowned at them both. Why was it that older kids were always crazier than younger ones? Pain wagged his tail and dribbled in anticipation.

"My dad lets me eat what I want," Luffy boasted as he tried to flatten his wiry, fair hair with his free hand. "He made these chips when he got back from night shift. I don't know why, but they taste much better wrapped in newspaper."

Anjuli giggled.

"You're going all silly!" Pete said.

"Am not!" Anjuli gave him a filthy look.

"By the way," Luffy pretended not to know what they were talking about. "What was your report like?"

"Oh... , OK," Anjuli tried to act normal. "You keep that killer dog away from me!"

"Pain just wants a chip!" Pete laughed. "He's not going to hurt you."

"Here," Luffy threw Pain three chips. He caught each one in mid-air.

"Mine was great," Luffy grinned, his wiry hair standing on end again. "Mr Williams said I was one in a million when it came to numbers."

"What does that mean?" Anjuli said, "You know how sarcastic he is."

"That I'm brilliant at maths!" Luffy snarled and scoffed two large chips at once.

"What mark did you get for the test?"

Anjuli asked.

"Er…" Luffy looked away. "I'm not very good at tests!"

"Well?" Anjuli stared him straight in the eye. "How many per cent?"

"Let's see," Luffy ate the last chip, screwed up the newspaper and flattened his wiry hair again with his hand. "What was it now?"

"Huh!" Anjuli sniffed. "It's not something you forget. Unless…"

"What did you get then?" Luffy said.

"Eighty-six… no, hang on, it was eighty-seven per cent for maths," Anjuli grinned up at the sky. "Beat that!"

"Really?" Luffy's face sank. His hair sprang up. "Well, I'm not that good at maths if you must know. I'm better at geography."

"Come on," Pete was getting bored. "Let's go and get the sticky tape."

"What time should I come round for tea?" Luffy looked depressed. He didn't want to meet Anjuli's eyes. She was grinning from ear to ear. "About three?"

"Yeah," Pete had already walked off.

"I'll help you with your maths if you like." Anjuli couldn't resist saying it. "Really, I don't mind." She winked.

"Sure," Luffy grunted crossly. "That's all I need!"

Pete burst out laughing when Anjuli caught up with him.

"You're no good at maths!"

"Who says?" Anjuli was shocked. "Sarky Williams knows nothing."

"Yeah?" Pete smiled. "I heard your mum telling you off this morning. Your window was wide open."

"That was nothing to do with maths!"

Anjuli said quickly. "She was cross because I hadn't washed up and I spilt her nail varnish on the…"

"OK, OK," Pete held his hands up and surrendered. Anjuli was impossible to argue with. "Why are you walking three paces behind me?" he shouted.

"Do you think I'm going to catch rabies from that killer dog?" Anjuli shouted back. "You can, if you like. And for the last time, I don't fancy Luffy!"

"Yeah, OK," Pete said, "and for the last time, this is not a killer dog." He began tying Pain up to the lamp post outside Hossenbux's Corner Shop. "You're mad, you are!"

Behind the counter of the shop, instead of the ever-grinning, quick-moving Mr Hossenbux smiling them a welcome, a crumpled figure bent over a telephone.

"There's nothing I can do," Mr Hossenbux waved his head sadly as he spoke into the receiver. "I'm sorry, but that's how it is."

Anjuli and Pete looked at each other, wondering what on earth had gone wrong for nice Mr Hossenbux. He nodded to them, put the phone down and sighed heavily.

"It's hopeless," he said to the rows of packaged sweets lined up on the counter.

"What is?" Anjuli had to know what had happened.

"The Inter-School Maths Challenge," Mr Hossenbux frowned. "My Simon had set his heart on winning it for the school. And now he's been rushed to hospital with appendicitis. He's so upset he's let everyone down! The challenge is happening at twelve o'clock at the Town Hall. What are they going to do without my clever Simon, the best maths student in Westcot Green school?"

"You're so lucky!" A loud voice shouted from behind them.

Pete looked round. Anjuli looked round. Luffy stood at the door grinning from ear to ear. "Anjuli got eighty-six, no eighty-seven per cent in the maths test. She can do the quiz instead."

A small smile crossed Mr Hossenbux's face. He clapped his hands. "A miracle!"

"You what?" Anjuli nearly passed out. "I'm helping Pete with his birthday tea this afternoon. His mum's in bed with flu."

"And we've got urgent repairs to do," Pete said.

"What urgent repairs?" said Luffy innocently.

Pete scowled at Anjuli. "Er, just something to do with a door."

"I'm busy today!" Anjuli said quickly. "Sorry."

"But you're the maths wizard now Simon's in hospital, Anjuli," Luffy said. "Who else from Westcot Green School can do it but you?"

"True," Anjuli grinned at the very idea of being thought a wizard at anything. "I am pretty brilliant at maths, everyone knows that, but…"

"Thank you, Anjuli. That will make me feel so much better." Mr Hossenbux rushed to the phone.

"Hang on…" Anjuli stared in horror. "I can't…"

Mr Hossenbux ignored her and quickly dialled the number.

"Hello," his eyes sparkled. "Yes, it's me. Thank heavens the problem's solved. We have another very good competitor willing to take my Simon's place. A girl. Anjuli's her name. She'll be there by twelve."

"Wait!" Anjuli shouted, "It's imposs—"

"Be there by a quarter to twelve," Mr Hossenbux said, putting the phone down. "Take the first door on the right inside the Town Hall, and someone will meet you. Probably someone from the local radio station. I must go to the hospital now to see how my Simon's getting on. Can you children please hurry up? I want to close up the shop."

Anjuli tried to speak, but no words came out of her mouth. Pete paid for the sticky tape and some blue stuff and pulled her out of the door by the elbow.

"What's wrong with you?" Luffy said. "You look as if you're going to be sick."

"I can't do it," Anjuli whispered, white as a sheet.

"Yeah, you can," Luffy said. "You got nearly ninety per cent."

"No!" Anjuli was almost in tears. "I... I... see, I..."

"She's hopeless at maths," Pete said. "Ask anyone."

"How come?" Luffy said. "You got eighty-seven per cent in the test?"

"It was a fluke. One of those things..."

"No!" Luffy shook his head. "I only got thirty-four per cent!"

"What?" Anjuli stopped in her tracks. "That's the worst mark I've ever heard. You'd better give it up."

"Yeah, I know," Luffy sighed. "But I didn't come last. There were three others lower than me. I wish I knew who they were. Do you know?"

"Me?" Anjuli gave him a look that could spread diseases. "I don't hang about with failures."

"No, 'course," Luffy hung his head. "I was just wondering who was worse at maths than me, that's all."

"Wait," Anjuli had an idea. "Romesh is good at maths."

"Is he?" Luffy tried to sound interested. "I expect he'll know who came last. He knows about everyone."

"That's not what I'm talking about!" Anjuli shouted.

"So?" Luffy looked confused. "What are you saying then?"

"Yeah," Pete began untying Pain from the lamp post. "So what?"

"Romesh can..." a strange smile crossed Anjuli's face. She bit her lip. "Yeah, that's it."

"Romesh can what?" Luffy licked a

sparkle of chip salt from his hand then flattened his wiry hair.

"He can do the quiz instead of me," Anjuli said. "He'll have to dress up as a girl, of course."

"Whaaaa?" Pete nearly fell over. "You're mad. Why would Romesh do that?"

"Just tell them you don't want to do it." Luffy said. "That'll sort it. There's nothing wrong with being scared stiff."

"Huh!" Anjuli looked furious. "I'm not scared of anything."

"Tell the truth," Pete pleaded. "We've got to do the door!"

"That can wait!" Anjuli wasn't going to be stopped that easily. "It'll be a laugh. Everyone in the whole town will think I'm brilliant at maths, even Sarky Williams. And Romesh, he won't mind."

"But everyone thinks you're brilliant at maths because of what you got in the test," Luffy was baffled. "I don't get it."

"Stop being boring!" Anjuli silenced him.

Pete sighed. Anjuli flashed them both a

deadly smile. "Remember what Romesh did?"

Luffy and Pete both shook their heads.

"It was him who invented Inside-Out Day to raise money for that charity," Anjuli said.

"Oh," Pete remembered that all right. He'd had to spend the day in infant school walking round with his underpants and vest on outside his school tracksuit, thanks to Romesh. And Pips Westwood in her gran's purple baggy knickers! He still couldn't get that awful picture out of his mind.

"Let's have some fun!" Anjuli said. "Come on!"

"Romesh is even madder than you, Anjuli!" Luffy said. "It'll be a right laugh!"

"What about the door?" Pete said. "What's more important?"

"There's loads of time. Stop worrying." Anjuli strode ahead towards the street where Romesh lived. "The birthday tea isn't until three."

"What's the problem with the door?" Luffy loped along beside Pete, Pain in between them, sniffing their knees.

"Never mind." Pete couldn't be bothered to explain and he sulked all the way to Romesh's house. By the time they reached Willow Lane, Anjuli was already knocking on the door of number fifty-two.

"Hi!" good-looking Romesh opened the door wide. "Hey, Anjuli, what's happening?" He smoothed his black, glossy hair back, as if he was being filmed.

"Want to do something mad?" she asked. "You'll enjoy it, promise!"

Romesh glanced at Luffy and Pete. "Are they doing it?"

"No, silly," Anjuli grinned. "Only you!"

"What, then?" he asked. Anjuli covered her mouth with her hand and whispered in his ear.

"I was going to go swimming!" Romesh said, his big brown eyes twinkling with the mad idea of doing a quiz dressed up as Anjuli, whom he'd always liked. "Why should I?"

"Er…" Anjuli tried to think. "Go on, it'll be a laugh! I'll lend you my blue skirt and blue nail varnish. You'll look good in it. Better than me."

"No, thanks!" Romesh said.

"You can come to Pete's birthday tea," Luffy said.

Pete, Anjuli and Romesh groaned.

"Nah!" Romesh wasn't going to be bought that cheaply. "I'd rather go swimming."

"Wait," Anjuli said. "We can all go swimming later!"

"No, we can't," Pete shouted. It's my birthd—"

"Good idea," Luffy said. "I fancy going swimming later, only I haven't got any money."

"All right," Anjuli sounded impatient. "I'll pay for everyone."

"OK, then," Romesh said. "Count me in."

"And me," Luffy smiled.

"Huh?" Pete was amazed. "You haven't got any money to take everyone swimming. I had to pay for the sticky tape because you didn't have any money."

"I've got loads of money!" Anjuli glared at him. "I just didn't have any on me at that exact moment. Honestly, I don't know why you're

always trying to stop everything."

"OK," Romesh's face lit up. "Let's go."

Anjuli grinned from ear to ear.

Pete's mouth fell open. "This is supposed to be my birthday! When are we going swimming?"

"Not now!" Anjuli said crossly. "Don't you understand anything?" She bent over and whispered in Pete's ear. "I only said that to Romesh to get him to do the quiz."

"Oh!" Pete sucked air through his tombstone teeth. "Just so long as I know."

"By the way, Romesh," Luffy said. "What did you get in the maths test?"

"Seventy-one per cent," Romesh curled his top lip. "Not bad, eh?"

"Could have been a lot better," Anjuli said. "Still, never mind. Better luck next time. Come on, we've got things to do."

"She got higher than y—" Luffy wasn't allowed to say anymore. Anjuli nudged her elbow sharply into his side.

"Yow! that hurt," Luffy bent over. "Why did you do that?"

"Boys don't like coming lower than girls in tests." Anjuli whispered. "Why upset him? It'll just ruin his day and then he won't want to be me in the Maths Challenge."

"I get it," Luffy smiled. "You were happy to ruin *my* day telling me your result, but not Romesh. Oh, no, not him."

"Yeah," Anjuli had to admit. "But you can take it, Luffy. Romesh is much more sensitive. You know how he is." Anjuli ran up to Romesh, who had taken Pain's lead and was being pulled along the street faster than he could walk. Pete was running alongside.

"I'm VERY SENSITIVE!" Luffy shouted. "It's just that no one knows!"

4

Wonky!

"You're not putting those in my hair!" Romesh held his hands up to stop Anjuli curling a roller round his long straight locks. "No way. Get off."

Luffy fell off Anjuli's sofa in a fit of giggles.

"Your hair's too straight," Anjuli sighed. "It'll look more like mine with a bit of a kink."

"Yeah, it will," Pete had just arrived, after taking Pain home.

"Shut up, you," Romesh said as he turned to face Pete.

"Leave him alone," added Anjuli, pinning a roller in. "It's his birthday today."

They all looked at Pete for a second.

"Yeah," Pete straightened his shoulders as he leaned against the living room door. "You've all got to be nice to me!"

Suddenly the back door opened with a bang.

"Quick! Hide," Anjuli whispered. "It's my mum. She must have come back for something."

Luffy dived over the top of the sofa, followed by a leaping Pete. Anjuli and Romesh each pulled a green curtain over them. A hush settled on the small living room as the door opened.

"Anjuli, do you think your shoes aren't showing?" Mum said quietly as Anjuli let out a sigh. "Why are you hiding?"

Anjuli swished the curtain aside and stepped out.

"And who's that?"

Romesh peered sheepishly out from the other side, a huge pink roller on the top of his head.

"What's going on?"

A giggle sounded from the back of the sofa.

"Will you please get out from there?"

Pete and Luffy popped up. Their smiles froze.

Mum folded her arms. "Why are there three boys in my living room at 10.30 in the morning, Anjuli?" she demanded.

"Er..." Anjuli thought hard. "Um..."

"We're planning my party," Pete piped up. "Mum's sick in bed and we didn't want to disturb her, so Anjuli said we could come here and…" It almost worked. Anjuli's mum nearly smiled, until her eyes went back to the pink roller on the top of Romesh's head.

"All the boys are going to the party dressed as girls and the girls are going dressed as boys," Luffy said matter-of-factly. A grin spread round the room faster than the speed of light.

"I see," Mum unfolded her arms. "Well, you can all get dressed somewhere else. Understand!" They all nodded and headed for the door. "Not you, Anjuli!"

"Why?" Anjuli turned round.

"I work hard every day," Mum began as soon as the front door had shut behind Pete, Luffy and Romesh. Anjuli had heard this speech a thousand times before. "I'm lucky to have a job at the estate agents round the corner. That means I can pop home every now and then to make sure you're OK." Anjuli stared at the rose-patterned carpet. "I don't want anyone else in the house when I'm not here. Do you understand?"

Anjuli nodded.

"I'll be home at lunchtime."

Anjuli nodded again.

"And I don't expect to see half the street in here when I come back!"

"Yes," Anjuli sighed. She'd realized long ago that the quieter she kept when Mum was cross, the sooner the speeches ended. "Sorry!"

"I'm needed at work," Mum walked to the door. "Now try and behave yourself for the rest of the day. See you at one."

Anjuli nodded, hoping the Inter-School Maths Challenge would be finished by then.

As soon as the coast was clear, she ran next door to Pete's house with a bag of her best clothes. She found Romesh, pink curler still on the top of his head, lying on the kitchen floor with a hammer in his hand. Luffy stood beside him scratching his wiry hair and Pete was making dents in a ball of blue sticky stuff with both thumbs.

"What's happening?" Anjuli gasped.

"He's mending the door properly," Pete said as Romesh hammered a blue plank across the gap.

"Honestly!" Romesh hissed through the three nails lined up between his teeth. "This door's all skew-ways!"

"Skew-ways? Don't be daft. It's skew-with," Luffy said. "Not skew-ways! There's no such word as skew-ways!"

"The word's skew-whiff, you idiots," Anjuli said. "Don't you know anything?"

"Skew-whiff? I don't think so... That's the stupidest word I've ever heard," Luffy laughed. "It's skew-*with*, I'm telling you."

"Ha?" Romesh spat out a nail. "You mean skew-*ways*!"

"Can you please stop arguing?" Pete said. "Why can't you just say wonky?"

"Skew-whiff," Anjuli said. "Same thing! And where did you find that blue plank?"

"It was under my bed," Pete said. "Look! When Romesh is finished you won't even notice there's a hole."

"Apart from the fact that the plank is blue

and the door is plain wood," Luffy added. "And nails are sticking out everywhere, and it's all skew-thingy, whiffy, wonky."

"Exactly." Anjuli was itching to get her hands on the hammer. It made her feel ill to see Romesh having all the fun. "Give it to me."

She grabbed the hammer from him and started pulling out the nails with the twin things the other side of the hammer. Twin things she'd always wanted to use.

"You're so bossy, you!" Romesh got up from the floor. The nails flew across the kitchen one by one.

"Why don't you just get another door?" Luffy asked. Romesh, Anjuli and Pete stared at him as if he'd gone mad. "Well? I don't understand," he added.

"Your ideas aren't helping," Anjuli said. "You better keep quiet."

Luffy shut up.

"There you go." Anjuli sat back with the blue plank safely in her arms. There was something about this woodwork thing that made her feel so happy. "Now give me back the scarf."

Luffy handed it to her and she stuck the scarf back on the bottom of the door. "That's much better. We can make something good out of that plank later," she said to Pete. "Let's get Romesh ready for the quiz."

"Do we have to?" Pete said, making that sucky sound with his teeth. "I'd really like to get the door sorted now."

"We've got loads of time after the quiz. Come on," Anjuli pulled Romesh out of the kitchen. "Hurry up, will you?"

Luffy and Pete had no other choice but to follow her.

* * *

Half an hour later, Romesh appeared at the bathroom door dressed in a straight denim skirt, a white blouse and tights. The scuffed black shoes belonging to Anjuli's mum were a bit of a squash and had a hint of a heel, which made him wobble.

"Well?" He flashed his stubby blue finger nails at them. "Does the colour go with my eyes?" Luffy burst into hysterics. Romesh kicked a heel in the air like a dancer.

"What a dork!" Luffy screamed.

"He looks great!" Anjuli said, as Romesh flicked his bouncy, curled hair behind his ears. "But you should have shaved your legs while you were in there."

They all stared at the black hairs curled and flattened by the white tights.

"No one will notice," Pete said. "He really does look a bit like you, Anjuli."

"Let's go then," Anjuli smiled. "The Town Hall."

She put her arm through Romesh's and they walked together down the street. "We're twins," Anjuli said, ignoring the giggles coming from Pete and Luffy behind, who were imitating Romesh's awkward walk.

"Try to lift your feet!" Anjuli advised, "instead of scraping the pavement off."

"How can girls go round like this?" Romesh took some tiny steps. "I feel stupid. This skirt's so straight I'm going to fall over."

"Stop moaning!" Anjuli elbowed him in

the side. "You're enjoying it."

Romesh had to admit it felt nice to have Anjuli's arm through his.

"Why haven't I got a push-up bra?" Romesh suddenly said. Anjuli bumped him off the pavement into the road. "Or some nice pink knickers?" he couldn't help adding.

"I don't think so." Anjuli pretended to smile. "Pink's not your colour."

"We'll get you some fancy knickers!" Luffy shouted.

Pete giggled, "They'd look great under your school shorts."

"Like this!" Romesh said in a high pitched voice and walked off, swaying his hips like a model on a catwalk. Anjuli, Pete and Luffy laughed all the way to the town centre and up the steps of the Town Hall.

It wasn't until they were inside the marble entrance that Romesh began to have second thoughts.

"All entrants sign in here." A jolly man with a ginger beard called them over to his desk. Romesh thought about bolting back out of the revolving doors, but Anjuli pulled him towards the signing-in book. She pointed at the space reserved for late entrants.

"I... er..." Romesh suddenly knew he couldn't go through with this.

"He's nerv— I mean she's nervous." Anjuli smiled at the ginger beard. He smiled back and passed Romesh a pen.

"Don't be shy, lass."

"Err," Romesh looked at Anjuli for help.

"Sign it," Anjuli said under her breath. "And don't write *your* name."

Romesh did as he was told. He wrote 'Anjuli Sansoni' and when he looked up he saw Pete and Luffy doubled up, clutching their stomachs.

"This way, lass," the man pointed towards the entrants' door. Romesh gave Pete and Luffy a filthy look. He didn't like being called 'lass'.

"Good luck," the ginger-bearded man said and Romesh just stood there.

"Go on," Anjuli hissed. "He means you."

Romesh suddenly jerked round.

"Go through that door, lass," the ginger beard said. "All the other entrants are in there. The rest of you can go through the last door on the left and find a seat."

"Um... I.... ah...," Romesh shivered as they headed down the hall. "I need the loo!" he muttered to Anjuli under his breath.

"Over there," Anjuli pointed at the ladies toilet and tried not to laugh. "Go on," she gave him a little push.

At that moment Romesh spotted the lovely Carla Wake outside the loo door. She was sliding her long brown hair into an elastic band.

"Hey," she waved at Anjuli, stopping for a second to look Romesh up and down. "Didn't know you had a sister. Are you going to watch the competition?"

"Yeah," Anjuli shrugged, wishing the

ground would open and swallow up Carla. "That's right."

Carla nodded. Anjuli looked away. If there was one person in the whole world she hated it was Carla fakey Wakey. Not that Carla had ever really done anything to her. It was just the way she looked at you with that false smile and eyes as cold as ice.

"See you inside," Carla pouted at the ceiling and walked off flicking her pony tail from side to side.

"Whoar," Romesh said as she walked off. "Isn't she beauti—"

Anjuli stopped him with a little shove. "Hurry up! It'll be starting any minute."

"Nah," Romesh folded his arms. "Not in a million years am I going in there."

The sight of the lovely Carla Wake had brought him to his senses. "I'm not putting up with this rubbish! I'm off. See you later!"

"Romesh," Anjuli whispered through clenched teeth, "don't be stupid." She clutched his elbow tight. "The whole school's relying on you."

Romesh pulled his arm away. "Sorry!" he said. "But I'm not enjoying this. See ya!" He hitched up his skirt and dashed for the revolving doors.

"I'll never speak to you again," Anjuli shouted. "And your boxer shorts are showing!"

A number of startled people watched Romesh skid into the doors, skirt clutched round his waist. His boxer shorts were squashed up like folded flags underneath his white tights. The ginger-bearded man raised his eyes as if to ask a question.

"He's forgotten her earrings!" Anjuli said as Romesh disappeared down the steps like a whirling tornado. Carla Wake turned round, her eyes half-popping out of her head, then burst out laughing.

"Dorkhead," Luffy explained.

"Can we go home now?" Pete asked. "Please, it is my birthday!"

"Shush!" Anjuli gasped and quickly held

her hand up to stop Pete saying anything else. "It's not possible." An icy shiver ran down her back like a slithering snake. It couldn't be!

She watched, hypnotized, as the huge Town Hall doors swung round… to reveal the last person in the whole universe she wanted to see.

5

In Her Dreams

"No!" Anjuli whispered to the heavens above. "Not him."

"Hi, Mr Williams," Luffy smiled at the teacher who nodded a quick hello. "Come to watch the Inter-School Maths Challenge?"

"No," Mr Williams bit the side of his lip. "I've come to see the gymnastics tournament. Silly boy!" Luffy's smile fell away. He stepped back to avoid another put-down.

"There you are, Anjuli Sansoni!" Mr Williams said crossly. "I've just been round to your house. Couldn't find you anywhere."

"Uh… er…" Anjuli stuttered.

"You've had it now!" Pete said. "You're dead!"

"Thank goodness," Mr Williams put both hands in his crumpled jacket pockets, "Mr Hossenbux had the intelligence to phone me and give me the astonishing news that my worst maths pupil is to take his son's place in the Inter-School Maths Challenge."

"But," Luffy interrupted, "Anjuli got eighty-seven per cent in the test!"

"In her dreams, lad!" Mr Williams sighed. "In her wildest dreams!"

"You *didn't* get eighty-seven per cent?" Luffy widened his eyes. "You told me!"

"I…" Anjuli racked her brains for a reason to explain her lie. "I could have got two hundred per cent, if you must know," was all she could come up with in the time allotted.

"You'd better come with me right now, girl," Mr Williams said. "The quiz has luckily been postponed for half an hour, which may just give us time to sort a few things out."

"What things?" Anjuli said.

"Come on, young lady!" Mr Williams said, marching her off down the hall.

"Hey," Anjuli called to Pete and Luffy. "Don't go! Wait for me."

"All right, all right," Luffy said. "Don't panic. We'll be here to sweep up your body."

Anjuli pulled a face as she disappeared down the corridor.

"How many per cent did she get for the maths test then?" Luffy asked.

"Dunno," Pete shrugged. "But she told me she got ninety-nine per cent for Latin and she's going to a school for genius kids next year."

"So you think she's lying then?" Luffy asked.

"Our school doesn't do Latin," Pete gave him a worried look. "Does it?"

"Not sure," Luffy said. "I'm in the bottom group for everything except geography. I bet there's a secret Latin class and no one's even bothered to tell me about it."

"Yeah, right!" Pete said. "I'm off. My birthday tea's at three."

"Hang on!" Luffy grabbed his arm. "Let's

get a seat and see what happens. It'll be a laugh. Come on, we promised to wait."

"So what? It's my birthday. The kitchen's a mess. Part of the door's missing," Pete moaned. "We haven't started making the food and my mum's probably out looking for me even though she's sick and..."

"Never mind all that," Luffy said, waving away all Pete's problems with a few large swipes at the air above his head. "We can sort it out later. This'll be a laugh," he said in exactly the same manner as Anjuli.

"Why does everyone always do what she wants?" Pete asked.

"You should know," Luffy grinned.

Pete followed Luffy to the busy room on the right where the spectators' seats were filling up. They found two chairs in the fourth row and sat down. Pete crumpled forwards on his elbows, head hung low. He was so fed up he started counting the criss-crosses on the waxed floor beneath his feet. He lost his place, counting some wooden panels twice and forgetting where he started. It was no joke hanging round with Anjuli.

"And why are you at the Inter-School Maths Challenge?" Luffy raised his head to see a very spotty man with a microphone standing over him.

"Er..." Luffy grinned, "there's nothing else to do." The spotty man curled his face with bored contempt.

"And you?" he stared at Pete. "Remember we're on air!" he mouthed. "Try and say something different!"

Pete thought about leaping to his feet and running off. Instead, he sat up straight. "I've been tricked!"

The spotty man leaned forward and whispered, "Explain yourself. Go on. Speak clearly." He nodded to the sound man behind him.

"Well, you see," Pete began, glad to have the chance to tell the world how he'd been swindled out of a great day. "Today's my birthday and Anjuli said she'd come and help me get the food ready because my mum's sick and Anjuli liked my present so much she..."

"And that was one of the members of the audience," the spotty man spoke into the microphone and turned round to face the stage and sound man. "This young man is so excited about the Inter-School Maths Challenge that's he's decided to spend his birthday here in the Town Hall."

"NO!" Pete leaped out of his chair. He shoved his furious face in the microphone. "That's not it!" he screamed.

"Shut up!" the spotty man exploded with a stifled whisper. The sound man waved Pete back to his seat.

"That was cool!" Luffy patted Pete on the shoulder. "Everyone in the whole town heard you."

"And now, listeners!" the spotty man said in a sickly voice. "It's one minute to go and all the members of the panel are gathering on stage to begin the quiz."

Pete and Luffy looked up. Six serious kids of various shapes and sizes were shambling around, looking for their place cards and waiting to be told what to do next. Suddenly, Anjuli walked on stage swishing her slippery hair out of her eyes with both hands. She stopped for a second and looked out at the audience.

"We're over here!" Luffy stood up and frantically waved his rake-thin arms. Anjuli nodded and clutched her neck with her fingers, letting her head fall back and her tongue loll out to show how she was about to die. The packed audience burst out laughing. Anjuli bowed and walked to her seat without a care in the world.

Mr Williams sat in the front row with his head in his hands as the challenge began.

"Welcome, everyone," a posh man in a dark suit announced from the podium at the

side of the stage. "Each school is represented by a single member. This year we are proud to have seven schools taking part. The rules are as follows:

Members of the panel must press a buzzer to answer.

The first buzzer pressed will take the question. All working out to be done on the paper in front of you.

There is no conferring.

The winning school will gain a computer and thirty pounds for the contestant.

The second school will win two educational software programmes and fifteen

pounds for the contestant.

Anjuli's eyes widened. There was money to be won? It was the first she'd heard of it. Why hadn't anyone mentioned it? She wished now more than anything, she'd listened in maths.

Suddenly, a small nervous man came up to the man on the podium and said something. A woman hurried over with a piece of paper. Mr Williams looked up.

The posh man on the podium sighed. "I'm sorry to have to tell you that the challenge is delayed by another forty minutes as the Mayor is still caught in a traffic jam."

"No!" Pete screamed. Everyone looked

round, startled at the terrifying sound he'd made. Luffy put his hand over Pete's mouth to shut him up. A grumble of discontent rumbled round the room. Chairs scraped the floor.

Anjuli dashed from her seat, ran up to Mr Williams and gasped, "This time I'll listen. Promise!"

Mr Williams gazed at her frowning face. "I beg your pardon?"

"I didn't care before, but now I do," Anjuli pleaded. "Teach me everything you know. We've got just over half an hour!"

"Anjuli, I've just spent half an hour trying to help you while you stared out of the window singing mindless pop songs," Mr Williams looked away. "I'd rather teach a donkey to fly!"

6

YOU DID OOO–DID–OOO!

"Aw, sir," Anjuli grabbed his arm. "Please!" She sat down beside him and stared at his unhappy face. "I can do it! Give me a chance."

"Really," Mr Williams stared into the distance, "do I look like the kind of person who enjoys being made a fool of?"

"No, sir," Anjuli said. "But this time it'll be easier than teaching a donkey to fly. Promise!"

"Is that so?" He didn't bother to look at her. "And why is that, exactly?"

"Because I want the prize money," Anjuli said firmly. "You didn't tell me there was money in it!"

"Ah yes!" Mr Williams snorted. "Silly old me for not understanding! Of course, now it's worth listening isn't it?"

Anjuli nodded very fast. He was catching on, thank goodness.

"Prime numbers don't do anything?" Anjuli said very quickly. "See, I know something."

Mr Williams almost got up and walked away. But something made him stop and turn towards her. "OK, explain quickly why thirteen is a prime number."

"Er..." Anjuli racked her brains. "I know it, I do."

"Well?" Mr Williams sighed.

"Because you can't multiply it and it doesn't divide by anything," Anjuli gabbled.

"Prime numbers can't be divided by anything. Yes, that's right," Mr Williams said slowly. "And the only way to get a prime number is to multiply one by the number itself. One times thirteen is..."

Anjuli nodded. "Thirteen. I get it."

Very carefully, he went through fractions and percentages, square roots and decimals, number patterns and sequences and Anjuli listened hard. Every last molecule in her brain paid attention to him. Instead of her usual classroom-thinking where she made plans to persuade a space craft to kidnap Sarky Williams and leave him in the outer atmosphere, she listened to every word he said.

Bit by bit the clouds lifted. Anjuli could feel her brain tossing numbers around like a computer. Why had she thought maths was hard? This wasn't difficult. It wasn't even boring.

"Here, have this." Luffy handed a fizzy drink to Pete, who was slumped down in his seat. "Happy Birthday!"

Pete let out a grunting sound.

"Stop worrying," went on Luffy. "We'll be back in no time. It's only half past one. This is going to be hilarious."

"Is that why I'm laughing my head off? Ha ha ha!" Pete pushed the drink away and stood up. "I've had enough!"

"Hey," Luffy pulled him back and put his arm round his shoulder.

"This is the worst birthday I've ever had!" Pete said.

"Calm down," Luffy tried. "Trust me. Why don't you just buy another door?"

Pete glared at him.

"Sit down," Luffy said. "Anjuli will be back in a minute!"

"Do you fancy her?" Pete asked. "You never take your eyes off her."

"Me?" Luffy handed him the fizzy drink

again. "I don't know what you're on about."

Pete took the can and began to sip. "Don't you? Well, that door better be mended."

"It will," Luffy winked. "No problem!"

"Anjuli's better at coming up with ideas than you are," Pete said. "At least she manages to make me believe she's got a plan. You're only saying no problem because you don't want to sit here by yourself."

"Give over. It's starting," Luffy pointed at the stage. "Look!"

Pete looked up to see the same man take his place on the podium and tap the microphone. The room hushed. People found their seats and sat down. The contestants wandered back. Anjuli leaped on the stage and ran to her chair, grinning wildly. Mr Williams in the front row folded his arms and whispered something to the heavens above.

When the contestants were ready, a camerawoman stepped forwards and told them all to smile for her. Everyone tidied their hair and put on their best face. Everyone except Anjuli. When the flash went off she poked out her tongue.

"Welcome, again. Sorry for the unforeseen delay!" the posh man said. "As I mentioned earlier, each school is represented by a single contestant."

At that, Anjuli clenched her fists, raised her arms in the air and bowed at the audience, who immediately clapped and burst out laughing.

"Show 'em, Anjuli," Luffy screamed.

"We'll save all that for the winner," the man said icily, giving Anjuli a filthy look. "Let's begin. You all know the rules."

Anjuli couldn't wait. Now she would show the whole world how brilliant she was. She couldn't understand why Mr Williams was sitting in the front row muttering to himself and looking so miserable.

"The first buzzer pressed takes the question!" the man said. "Ready?"

They all nodded eagerly, but no one nodded as eagerly as Anjuli, who'd never been in a competition or sat on a stage before. She was so thrilled to be there that for a moment

time stopped, jagged to a sudden halt, and she couldn't quite remember what she was supposed to be doing. All those eager faces gazing up at her, grinning warmly and egging her on turned to a bleary haze.

Questions were fired out. Buzzers were pressed. Cheers went up. Anjuli found it hard to think in this atmosphere. Her brain began to frizzle up. Soon it would be the size of a crisp. The smiley boy next to her kept shooting his eyebrows to the top of his head and grunting like a maniac. He didn't seem to know how weird he looked. Try as she might, Anjuli couldn't take her eyes off him. Then he dared to twist round and give her a smug smile.

Suddenly, Anjuli decided she'd had enough. It was time to join the game... time to multiply, divide and add as fast as she could.

"Go for it!" she told herself as the smiley boy from Riddington Grammar School pressed the buzzer again.

"Seventy-nine point five kilograms."

"Correct!" The man on the podium smiled.

"That's another twenty points to Riddington Grammar School who now have sixty and are in the lead!"

"Yey!" the supporters shouted from the auditorium. "Yes, yes, Riddington!"

Anjuli started to get annoyed with the smiley boy from Riddington Grammar. She wasn't the only one. The boy from James Street Comprehensive sitting next to her whispered something nasty under his breath.

Anjuli felt herself going very hot. She could hardly breathe. Then her finger touched the buzzer. It went off before anyone else had a chance. All eyes swivelled to stare at her.

"You pressed the buzzer. You must take the question or forfeit ten points!" The man on the podium said severely.

"£1.33," Anjuli said. "And I don't have ten points to forfeit!"

"Correct. That's twenty points to Westcot Green School."

"HOORAY!" Luffy stood up and waved his arms about wildly. Mr Williams blinked in astonishment.

"What is the sum of fifty-eight and sixty-four?" the man asked.

Anjuli's finger was still at the buzzer. She pressed hard. "One hundred and twenty two."

"Correct. That's forty points to Westcot Green School."

Out of the side of her eye Anjuli watched Carla Wake politely press her palms together.

"HA, HA." Luffy went mad. "YOU DID OOO-DID-OOO."

"If you buy goods for £4.28 and pay with a £10 note, how much..." Anjuli pressed the buzzer before he finished the question.

"£5.72," she said.

"Correct," the man said. "That's sixty points to Westcot Green School."

"Good on you!" Luffy cheered.

Anjuli was amazed how easy this was, once you got going.

"What is the square root of forty nine?"

"Seven," Anjuli answered immediately.

"That's eighty points to Westcot Green and now you have a bonus question with extra points because you've answered the last four questions in a row correctly!"

"Anjuli, Anjuli, Anjuli," Luffy slow-hand clapped her. "Westcot Green, yeah, yeah, yeah! Riddington Green are rubbish..."

"Stop showing me up," Pete whispered. "Everyone will know you fancy her now!"

But Luffy didn't care. "Come on, come on, come on," he hollered.

Anjuli felt a trickle of sweat slip down her forehead.

"If your watch says it's two fifty-five and it's fifteen minutes fast, what is the right time?"

"Er," Anjuli could see thousands of eyes staring at her. Mr Williams was urging her on from the front row by raising his eyebrows and twitching his lips. "Two forty," Anjuli hoped.

"Correct. That's one hundred and ten points to Westcot Green!"

Anjuli leaped up

"Whahay!" she shouted, stabbing the air with her clenched fists and doing a little Irish dance around the table. Not that she knew how to do an Irish dance, but the way she kicked her feet up and held on to her hips left no one in any doubt as to what she thought she was dancing. The other contestants looked startled as she high stepped past them. The crowd whooped. Luffy whistled. The man on the podium looked aghast. He didn't know where to put his face.

Then a real dancer in a blue dress jumped up from the front row and linked elbows. Eyes down, she led Anjuli into a complicated foot movement which Anjuli tried with all her might to follow. Two older girls climbed on to the stage and joined in. Someone at the back of the audience stood up and started singing a tune in a rich strong voice. The dancers flipped their feet into the air and twirled. Chaos ruled.

Eventually the man on the podium remembered he was in charge. "Everyone get back to their seats!"

The singer at the back stopped singing. Anjuli did one last knee jerk and raced back to her chair. The other kids quickly scrambled down from the stage.

"This Challenge," the man with the microphone screeched out, "is not finished."

Anjuli looked round happily. The boy next to her scraped his chair as far away from her as he could.

"You weren't quick enough!" Luffy told Pete. "We could have got up there with them."

"You what?" Pete sighed.

"Any more unconventional behaviour from a contestant," the man said through grinding teeth, "and you'll be disqualified. Understand?"

Anjuli nodded, wondering why he was making such a fuss.

"There are two more questions!"

The contestants groaned in a defeated way.

The boy from Riddington Grammar looked as if he was about to throw up. Mr Williams squirmed in his seat.

19 - 4 = 15   19 - (4×2)
4×2 = 8   = 11

and   7   1·5 m (50 m)
                +2·5 m   50 cm
                1 · 75 cm
            5 - 1·60 cm
        5·1   1·55
9 = 1m 44 cm.

7

Brilliant

"Nineteen minus four times two?"

Three buzzers went off all in the same instant.

Anjuli's hand trembled. Time stood still, went backwards, somersaulted, did three loops and landed upside down. She saw the boy from James Street Comprehensive open his mouth to answer, heard the word, 'correct', without first taking it in. Her mind blanked out. Everything happened in front of her in slow motion. The man on the podium spread out his fingers. He nodded at the blonde boy next to her who tossed his head back, grinning so widely his exposed gums took up half his face.

"Twenty points to James Street Comprehensive!" the man said.

Anjuli stiffened uneasily.

"The last question is for fifty points!" he called.

"Whaaa?" Anjuli had to pull herself together, zero in on what was happening or lose! She focused her mind with all her might. "You can do it!" she told herself studying the deep marks her finger nails were gouging in the table. The clapping died away. The dust balls dancing in her eyes settled back. She listened closely to every word of the question.

"If Martin is one point seven five metres tall, Susan is fifteen centimetres shorter and her sister is five centimetres smaller than her, how tall is Gordon, who is eleven centimetres shorter than Susan's sister?" the man asked.

OH! NO! It was one of those!

Anjuli's brain tried to whizz, ziz, zizz... but it stopped all of a sudden. It hedged backwards, drooped, splurged all over the place and turned to lumpy custard instead.

"Less than fifteen her sister…Gordon. No…take away Susan from the…he's shorter by eleven…Who on earth is Martin?"

The boy from Riddington Grammar pressed the buzzer first.

"One point four four!"

"Correct. Fifty points to Riddington Grammar."

"NO!" Anjuli yelled.

"Yes," the man with the microphone said firmly. "Riddington Grammar School are this year's winners of the Inter-School Maths Challenge. They get a brand new computer and you, Jacob Barry, have won thirty pounds to spend as you wish."

A loud whoop went up in the audience.

"Second prize goes to Westcot Green School, who win two software programmes and you, Anjuli Sansoni, win fifteen pounds to spend as you wish."

The audience made a pounding noise with their feet. Luffy stomped up and down like a loony.

"Well done, well done," Mr Williams clapped hard as Anjuli came off stage. "You didn't make an idiot of the school after all. Though what you thought you were doing cavorting around the stage in the middle of it I don't know!"

"I was flying, sir," Anjuli smirked. "Like a donkey!"

"Ah," Mr Williams couldn't say much to that. "I see."

"I could have won, sir!" Anjuli said and he believed her.

"Hi," Carla Wake walked through the crowd, eyes fixed on the air above Anjuli's head. "You did well!"

"I did BRILLIANT!" Anjuli grinned.

It was getting dangerously late when Anjuli, Luffy and Pete left the Town Hall and began to make their way home to Elm Close. Anjuli held her money up to the sunlight to check it wasn't counterfeit.

"Everything has worked out fine for you," Pete complained. "My party's in half an hour and we haven't made any food or mended the door."

"I know where you can get a new pine door," Luffy said slowly as Anjuli strode off down the street towards home.

"You do?" In spite of everything, Pete couldn't help clutching at this straw of hope. "Where?"

"In my garage," Luffy said. "It's been there for years. My dad keeps wanting to sell it."

"Why didn't you say something before?" Pete exploded.

"I did, remember?" Luffy said. "You wanted to mend the door. I told you to get another—"

"You had a door in your garage all this time?" Anjuli turned round and looked at him.

"Yeah," Luffy said. "And it's yours for the bargain price of seven pounds!"

"What?" Anjuli said. "Fifty pence. That's all I'm prepared to pay."

"STOP IT," Pete screamed the loudest scream they'd ever heard. It stopped them both in their tracks. "We haven't got time to argue. IT'S TWENTY-FIVE TO THREE!"

"All right," Luffy said. "Relax! Seeing as it's your birthday you can have the door for six pounds, but don't forget, Anjuli, you're paying for us to go swimming later."

"Huh!" Anjuli argued all the way to Luffy's house. "No way."

After haggling for quite a while she handed Luffy four pounds.

"You're getting this for nothing!" Luffy told her as she grabbed a corner of the door and they all hauled it out of his dad's garage and carried it down the road to Pete's house. "I've just about given it to you."

At two minutes to three, having worked very hard, Anjuli, Luffy and Pete stood back to see the new door swinging back and forth over the tiled kitchen floor without making the smallest scratch.

"Phew!" Pete smiled. They threw the old door outside.

"I'll make something out of that later!" Anjuli said, rubbing her hands at the thought. Then she got to grips with the mountain of sandwich spreading.

Luffy made himself useful by pushing a heap of fudge bars together to make a fort cake.

Unfortunately it melted and looked more like a Christmas pudding by the time he had finished, but somehow he managed, after several attempts, to get all ten candles to stand up on top.

By a quarter to four, everyone had arrived and the party was in full swing.

Granny Vane handed Pete a new Country and Western CD. She demonstrated the latest line dancing steps on the living room carpet.

"Ged your pardners," she jigged. "One two three."

Pain flew after her trying to dig his teeth

into her white cowboy boots. Posh cousins, Phil and Jen, sat on the sofa and polished off all the cheese and cucumber sandwiches, then guzzled the peanut butter and gulped down a whole bottle of fizzy lemon drink each.

Moany uncle Chas didn't arrive, much to everyone's pleasure. Mum crawled down the stairs in her pink candlewick dressing gown to croak "Happy birthday" to Pete, who blew out all ten candles on his fort cake three seconds before the whole mound caved in.

Romesh turned up with a packet of custard creams, Anjuli's clothes in a bag, and a present.

"Thanks," Pete tore the paper off to reveal a red torch. "Just what I wanted," he smiled and scooped a large part of the sludge cake mess into his mouth. "That's the most scrumptious thing I've ever eaten!" he smacked his lips. They all dug their fingers in and agreed. "Yum, too right!"

"More people coming?" Luffy inquired. "Any girls?"

"Nah!" Pete said. "Everyone's here!"

All through the singing, dancing and eating, the sound of a gentle sawing could be heard outside in the yard. Suddenly the sound of hammering filtered into the house.

They all stepped outside.

"Well," Anjuli grinned, wiping her hands on her jeans. "What do you think?"

"Er..." Pete found it hard to express

himself. "It's a bit skew-whiff!"

"Love a duck!" Granny Vane said. "What have you been up to?"

"It's a kennel," Anjuli stood back proudly, "for Pain. When it's raining he won't get wet."

They all examined the shed-like object in front of them. Panels of door were nailed hopelessly to fence posts, cardboard was woven into the gaps. A bit of corrugated iron stood in place of a door. The whole grotto was large enough for a pony.

"Where did you get that blanket?" Pete pointed to the stripy blue material stretched out as a makeshift roof.

"Mum won't miss it!" Anjuli said. "Don't worry!"

"ANJULI!" Mum shouted as she tried to open the gate. "What's this thing doing in the way?"

"It's Pain's kennel," Anjuli froze. "I've just made it!"

"It seems you've had quite a day!" Mum gave up pushing and climbed over the gate. "I didn't get back at lunchtime to check on you, which was just as well, but I bumped into Mr Williams as I was leaving work and he told me everything. I must say I'm very impressed."

"She came second," Pete shouted.

Mum gave the roof of the kennel a strange look.

"That looks like my..." She stared at Pete who put on his innocent face.

She turned back to Anjuli. "Mr Williams said you had hidden depths and he's going to put you in the top maths group when you get back."

"Cor!" Luffy was amazed. "Lucky thing. They'll probably let you do Latin, too."

"Westcot Green doesn't do Latin!" Anjuli frowned.

"Well done!" Romesh patted her on the back. "Are we going swimming now?"

"Um... later!" A slow smile crept across her face. "Oh, your birthday present, Pete. It's in your bedroom!" Pete ran inside. Everyone crowded after him into the tiny room.

"Wow!" Pete shrieked. There on the floor was a computer games system.

"I hired it from the video shop," Anjuli laughed. "It's yours for three days. Happy birthday!"

Granny Vane turned off the Country and Western music and watched Pete, Luffy and Romesh attach leads to the television in the living room. Then she sat on the floor and joined in, shouting, "Kill, kill!" every few seconds.

While they played, Anjuli eyed up the blue plank. Taking the saw from the woodwork box she marked out suitable cuts for a bird table. Then she gripped the handle tight and, concentrating hard, gently pulled the blade back and forth...

About the author

I love funny books and I wanted to write one!

My older sister is the kind of girl who spent her childhood running through hedges away from bulls. She really did slice the bottom off the kitchen door and when she reminded me about it, we laughed 'til it hurt. I decided there and then to write a story about someone a bit like her.

Oh, oh... and when she reads this I'm going to be running through a few hedges away from her.